Rock, Rhythm and Rag
BOOK TWO

PIANO SOLOS

by Melvin Stecher, Norman Horowitz
and Claire Gordon

ISBN 978-0-7935-8574-8

G. SCHIRMER, Inc.

DISTRIBUTED BY

HAL•LEONARD®
CORPORATION
7777 W. BLUEMOUND RD. P.O. BOX 13819 MILWAUKEE, WI 53213

Copyright © 1977 by G. Schirmer, Inc. (ASCAP) New York, NY
International Copyright Secured. All Rights Reserved.
**Warning: Unauthorized reproduction of this publication is
prohibited by Federal law and subject to criminal prosecution.**

STECHER &
HOROWITZ
S&H
PIANO LIBRARY

BANDSTAND BOOGIE

With a boogie beat

HEAVY ROCK

With a steady rock beat

JOHNNY IN C

RED MAPLE RAG

In ragtime tempo

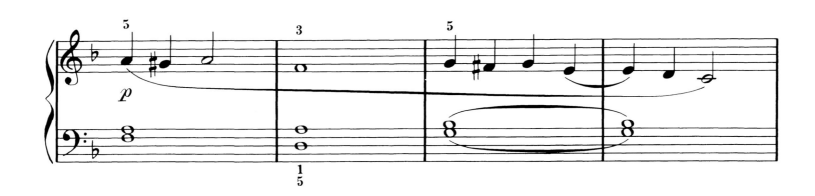

D.C. al Fine

ROCK SLIDE

With a solid rock beat

BLUESIANA

Moderate and steady blues

GLAD RAG

Spirited and bright

MILKY WAY SHAKE

With a swing and a bounce

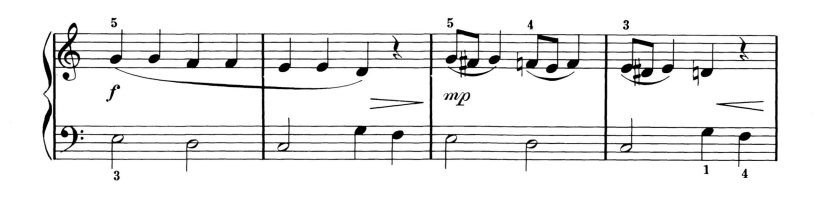

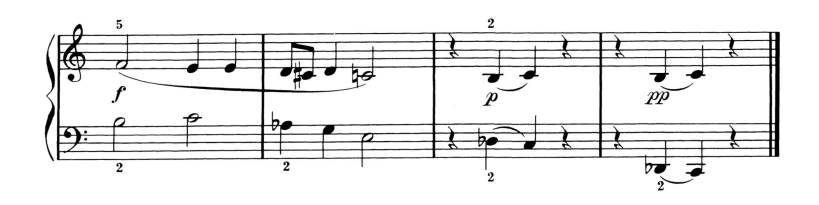

ROCK A LA MODE